"As a pastor's wife, I see how prayer[...] fights for the spiritual vitality of the [...] when a man or woman in our churc[...] gently questions him, and thanks him, because each time it is a cup of cold water to a thirsty soul. My husband always says, 'No one is suffering from too much encouragement.' Least of all our pastors. This book, if read and practiced, will not only be a blessing to your pastor (and his wife!), but will strengthen your entire church and community."

Christine Hoover, author, *How to Thrive as a Pastor's Wife*; host, *The Ministry Wives Podcast*

"A single preposition can make a world of difference! This book is entitled *Fight for Your Pastor* not *Fight Your Pastor*. Peter Orr wisely and winsomely helps us to see the *for* and then provides practical ways to make it a reality—and all with a touch of humor thrown in. Given everything that has unfolded for churches and their pastors in the last few years, this timely book will encourage church members to be faithful sheep as they seek to encourage faithful shepherds. The content carried even more weight for me since I personally know Peter as a Christian brother who has modeled a genuine love for Christ's church—for both its pastors and its people."

Jonny Gibson, Associate Professor of Old Testament, Westminster Theological Seminary; Teaching Elder in the International Presbyterian Church, United Kingdom

"It is to our advantage—to our own benefit and joy, says Hebrews 13:17— to have happy pastors, not groaning clergy. Of course, at the end of the day, the pastors' gladness and resilience is not the church's final responsibility. But we can pray for them. We can fight for them instead of against them. Joyless pastors plague the church! Dear God, make them truly, deeply happy and be pleased to use their congregants to be some small but real ingredient in their joy. Peter Orr's wise and timely book is a great place to start for how we can do our part."

David Mathis, Senior Teacher and Executive Editor, desiringGod. org; Pastor, Cities Church, Saint Paul, Minnesota; author, *Workers for Your Joy: The Call of Christ on Christian Leaders*

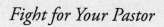

Fight for Your Pastor

Fight for Your Pastor

Peter Orr

Foreword by Dane C. Ortlund

WHEATON, ILLINOIS

Library of Congress Cataloging-in-Publication Data

Names: Orr, Peter, 1972- author.
Title: Fight for your pastor / Peter Orr.
Description: Wheaton, Illinois: Crossway, [2022] | Includes bibliographical references and index.
Identifiers: LCCN 2022005725 (print) | LCCN 2022005726 (ebook) | ISBN 9781433584763 (trade paperback) | ISBN 9781433584770 (pdf) | ISBN 9781433584787 (mobipocket) | ISBN 9781433584794 (epub)
Subjects: LCSH: Clergy. | Clergy—Prayers and devotions. | Clergy—Salaries, etc.
Classification: LCC BV4380 .O77 2022 (print) | LCC BV4380 (ebook) | DDC 248.8/92—dc23/eng/20220622
LC record available at https://lccn.loc.gov/2022005725
LC ebook record available at https://lccn.loc.gov/2022005726

Crossway is a publishing ministry of Good News Publishers.

BP		30	29	28	27	26	25	24	23	22
14	13	12	11	10	9	8	7	6	5	4	3	2	1

For Ben, Russ, Paul, Andrew, and Leo

Contents

Foreword

"FIGHT FOR YOUR PASTOR," this book is titled—not "Fight *with* Your Pastor." Pastors are just as fallible and fallen as any of us, yet the pressures they are under are unique and unremitting. Peter Orr sees what is at stake in the war zone of a pastor's heart and calls all of us to obey the New Testament and not just to tepidly receive our pastor's ministry, but also to proactively fight for his ministry, heart, and joy. He needs it.

A pastor is called to love, encourage, and build up his people. He must lead the way in this. But this will be a joy to him, and sustainable, only if the people self-consciously reciprocate that love and encouragement. Orr offers this important book out of a heart for the members of a church to hold up the hands of their spiritual leader, like Aaron and Hur holding up the hands of Moses (Ex. 17:12).

What kind of revival might break out if thousands of churches threw their arms around their pastors in the way this book prescribes? What we have here is the formula for apostolic Christianity itself—pastor and people loving and blessing one another, shepherd to sheep and sheep to shepherd, igniting a beauty of fellowship for which the world has no category.

Encouragement given is the glorious alternative to the common tragedy of withheld love and encouragement. Orr shows us how vital it is for a pastor's longevity in ministry for his people to receive his ministry *and to tell him they are receiving it*. Perhaps as churchgoers we think that it is enough not to criticize our pastor. It isn't. We must positively uphold him with life-giving words of specific and sincere encouragement. Our joy as members and his joy as a pastor are bound up with one another.

If he is such a poor pastor that you can't find anything to say to encourage him, then you need to find a new church. If you can find something to say, then you must. What you must *not* do is stay, saying nothing. Withheld love is a grievous failure; the devil smiles. For while overt or public criticism will end a man's ministry in the short term, the simple tragedy of withheld love will end a man's ministry in the long term. A ministry to silent parishioners is not sustainable.

I am deeply thankful for Peter Orr's exhortation for every church member to fight for their pastor. This is a wise book, and a needed one.

Dane C. Ortlund
Naperville Presbyterian Church
Naperville, Illinois

Introduction

*"Apart from other things, there is the daily pressure
on me of my anxiety for all the churches."*

2 CORINTHIANS 11:28

*"Is there a day that goes by when I don't
wonder how to get out of ministry?"*

AN ANONYMOUS PASTOR[1]

AS A SEMINARY professor in Australia, I have been involved
in training hundreds of men and women for ministry over
the last decade. A significant number of those who have
completed training and are in ministry—whether as senior
pastors, women's workers, or assistants—are facing personal,
psychological, or relational challenges. These difficulties

---

1   The quotes at the beginning of each chapter are from pastors whose names I have
    withheld. I have edited their comments slightly for grammar and clarity.

are so intense that many are leaving their posts—some to parachurch ministries, some to secular jobs, and some—tragically—leaving the faith altogether.

Two friends immediately come to mind. One recently wrote to me, "I always thought energy and optimism were my secret power—the thing that kept me from burnout. But here I am, struggling to function and on four weeks of medical leave to recover from it all. I'm not fully aware of what caused it. I think just the collective toll of a thousand difficulties and disappointments." Another pastor friend had to take medical leave because of some serious accusations made against him. He developed mouth ulcers, struggled to sleep, and was consumed with anxiety. After a year of intense stress, he was exonerated, but the effects remain with him and his family.

Of course, every Christian faces difficulty—Jesus called us to a life of carrying our crosses as we follow him. However, the challenges of those in pastoral ministry are often more acute. They have the same struggles as every Christian—following and living for Jesus in a world that hates him. However, they have the added role of leading other Christians who don't always want to be led and proclaiming the gospel to a world that does not want to hear. Being in Christian leadership has always been challenging, but recently it seems that the pressures have multiplied. Think of the difference between climate and weather. The "climate" for pastoral ministry is constant. The world, the flesh, and the devil are long-term climate factors that remain between Christ's first and second coming. But it feels as if—in the West, at least—there's been a change in the "weather." There is now a general weather front of apostasy, secularism, unbelief, and so on that is making the life of a pastor—particularly a conservative, complementarian, and evangelical one—more difficult.[2] Whether on matters of sexual ethics, gender, or the uniqueness of Christ, a faithful pastor who proclaims and stands for the word of God faces rising hostility from the world.

Pressure doesn't come only from outside. High-profile scandals have rocked the evangelical world, and these have raised questions about pastoral "power." Congregation members are wary—rightly so—of overbearing pastors. However, for every bullying or abusive pastor, there are many more who are seeking, however imperfectly, to faithfully lead our churches. But because of the failings of a few, even these godly men are now regarded with suspicion. It is hard to rebuke a congregation member (something Paul expects a pastor to do: Titus 2:15) when so many voices are proclaiming that pastors are drunk on power.

---

2   I am grateful to my friend Rory Shiner for this illustration.

The pressures caused by the recent pandemic further increased the pastor's burden. Many had to pivot quickly to online ministries. They were hit with criticism for not closing down quickly enough or for not opening up soon enough—or, conversely, for closing down in the first place. They faced the discouragement of congregation members continuing to stay away from church "because of COVID"—while happily attending restaurants, sporting events, and so on. A pastor friend of mine was complimented for his online resources since they enabled a family to "do church" at a more convenient time. Even better—by playing the service at 1.5 speed, "church took less time" out of the family schedule. With compliments like that, who needs criticism!

The Christian life was never meant to be easy. We follow a crucified Savior. Christian ministers have no monopoly on suffering. But in my experience and based on what the Scriptures say, pastors are the group under the most pressure. As Paul notes, "Apart from other things, there is the daily pressure on me of my anxiety for all the churches" (2 Cor. 11:28). Pastors' role in teaching the gospel and guarding congregations means they are under more extreme spiritual attack than the rest of us. Discouragement and opposition weigh heavily on them. Such spiritual opposition is part of the job, but it can be incredibly draining when it takes the form of unfair criticism or unrealistic expectation from believers.[3]

There is a crisis among pastors. As Christians, we can do little to change the prevailing "weather," but we can support our pastors as they lead us through stormy times. This short book is written as a call to more actively love and support our pastors. If you are reading this book, I am sure you love your pastor, but I want to nudge you to love him[4] more intentionally. I invite you to pause and think about how you can support him more. In short, I am calling you to fight for your pastor.

---

[3] Portions of this paragraph and others throughout the book are adapted from my article "Fight for Your Pastor," the Gospel Coalition, Australia edition, May 14, 2021, https://au.thegospelcoalition.org/. Used with permission.

[4] I am deliberately writing this book with respect to senior pastors, although I think the principles apply to others in full-time ministry. I want to concentrate on senior pastors because in my observation they are the ones who are under the most pressure—certainly in the contexts in which I live and work. For that reason, I have used the language of "he" throughout. I am convinced that the New Testament teaches that the role of the senior minister is reserved for men (e.g., 1 Tim. 2:12) even as it also affirms the vital ministry of women (e.g., Rom. 16:12; Phil. 4:3). If you disagree, I hope that you can still benefit from what I have written and apply it in your own context.

1

Fight!

"You also must help us by prayer."

2 CORINTHIANS 1:11

*"I wish my congregation would understand
that God would grow us to be more like Jesus
if we turned our criticism and cynicism into
prayer for others and church leaders."*

AN ANONYMOUS PASTOR

I COULD HAVE ENTITLED this chapter "Pray," but the idea of "fighting in prayer" (see 2 Cor. 10:4; Eph. 6:10–20) underlines the seriousness of the battle we need to undertake. The person who is under more satanic attack than anyone else you know is your pastor. The person whose faith Satan wants to derail the most is your pastor. The person whose marriage Satan would most like to wreck, whose kids he most wants to cause to rebel, whom he most wants to discourage is your pastor. You need to fight in prayer for your pastor.

It is striking how often the apostle Paul asks his churches to pray for him and his colleagues. In fact, it is striking that someone with such a clear grasp of God's sovereignty is so insistent that he *needs* the prayers of God's people. It is also instructive to consider the range of things that the apostle asks prayer for.

Paul outlines pressures he faced, describing how he "despaired of life itself" (2 Cor. 1:8). Thankfully, the Lord delivered him from these trials, but he is not naive enough to think that he will not face similar pressures in the future. He knows that the Lord will continue to deliver him, but he adds, "You also must help us by prayer" (1:11). Paul has seen the sovereign, miraculous deliverance of God in his life; nevertheless, he requests, commands even, the Corinthians to pray for him. He needs their help. Your pastor is not an apostle, but he needs you to help him by your prayers. He needs you to pray that he will endure even in the face of the kinds of pressure that might make him "despair of life itself."

Paul asks the Philippians to pray for his deliverance. Locked in a Roman prison, he tells the Philippians that he rejoices because he knows "that through your prayers and the help of the Spirit of Jesus Christ this will turn out for my deliverance" (Phil. 1:19). Paul is putting the prayers of Christians on the same level as the work of God! Of course, our prayers are so significant precisely because they ask *God* to work. Your pastor may not be in prison, but Paul expects that he will have to "endure suffering" (2 Tim. 4:5) if he is faithful to the gospel. The opposition that he faces can often feel too much to bear. He needs your prayers for deliverance and joy in the midst of trials.

Praying for your pastor has a double benefit. Primarily, when you pray for your pastor, you are asking our heavenly Father to work in his life. You are asking him to pour out his grace. You are asking for the supernatural help your pastor needs. However, there is a secondary benefit: praying for your pastor means that you are remembering him before the Lord (see Eph. 1:16 and 1 Thess. 1:3). To remember your pastor before the Lord means you are thinking about him in the presence of God, so you are less likely to be negative toward him. Spending more time remembering your pastor before the Lord means spending less time complaining about him to other people.

A Pastor Writes:

We have people who feel that they need to take a "time-out" from ministry serving because they are "struggling." We try to put on events that will help people to connect with others and remind them of the joys of the church family, but people feel too tired to commit. With all of that, we have a leadership team that is shouldering more and more responsibility and ministry tasks to help a Sunday gathering to happen. *They* are tired. I have walks with people from the church who are trying to keep work going, family going, who are not handling "life" as they might normally do, and it is never-ending. And then there is me. My mind is full of other people's problems, and I can't switch off. I have started to wake up and dread the day's to-do list. I am tired too, and it is a lonely place. I feel guilty asking others to do things when they have to take time to pray about it and then tell me that they can't, or that they will when things are more "normal."

A pastor recently shared with me what happened during a service he was hosting (because of local COVID restrictions) online. As the service began, the camera stopped talking to the computer and everything went off-line. It took nearly ten minutes to get back online. In that time, the pastor received two text messages. One came from a family that acknowledged how stressful this must be for him and said that the family members were praying for him. The other came from a frustrated church member wondering what was happening and pointing out how uncaring it was not to start on time. Pressure does funny things to people, but it would be great if our default instinct was to pray for our pastors rather than to criticize.

Often, Paul asks for prayer regarding his proclamation of the gospel—namely, that he would proclaim the gospel boldly (Eph. 6:18–20), clearly (Col. 4:4), and effectively (2 Thess. 3:1). A pastor is charged with doing the work of an evangelist (2 Tim. 4:5). This is a reminder that we can pray *positively* for our pastors, not just that they might endure the pressures and stresses they face, but also that they might diligently, boldly, and faithfully execute their ministries. Why not pray through the qualifications that Paul lays down for pastors in 1 and 2 Timothy and Titus? Why not pray that your pastor would be able to perform the duties and display the character that God expects of him?

Paul often starts his letters with short prayers for the churches he addresses. Why not pray through these prayers for your pastor? One of the most spiritually helpful things we can do is to pray through Scripture. As we read God's word and pray his words back to him, we can be confident that we pray according to his will. Paul's prayers are spiritually rich, varied, and detailed, so they will help us avoid bland "bless him" prayers.

A Pastor Writes:

I've recently had to discipline a couple over sexual sin and infidelity, and it's been the biggest ongoing source of stress; and yet, it would be totally inappropriate for me to share those details with someone who offers to pray for me. So I have to bear that burden quietly, and even though I want to share it for prayerful support, I can only speak in vague generalities to protect the privacy of others. In the end, it feels like no one is praying for me as I really want or need. I would love my congregation to understand that the very things I want and need prayer for are the very things I cannot share. When you genuinely ask how you can pray for me, please know that what I share is only a snapshot of the deeper things for which I truly want and need prayer. In fact, what I say might be so general and nonspecific that it appears totally meaningless! But that's because I can't get specific, because if I did, I would be inappropriately sharing the deep sins and struggles of other brothers and sisters in our congregation.

However, Paul can also issue a general request for the Thessalonian church to "pray for us" (1 Thess. 5:25). This prompts us to pray for our pastors in expansive terms. It doesn't take much to imagine what we could pray for them. In many ways, the prayers we pray for them are the same as those we pray for ourselves.

Here are some suggestions for prayers for your pastor:

- Pray for his marriage (if he is married)—that he would be a faithful husband.
- Pray for his kids—that they would grow up in the fear and knowledge of the Lord.
- Pray for his health—physical, mental, and spiritual.
- Pray that he would be wise in his use of technology—not giving in to impurity (pornography), time wasting (too much social media), or anger (again, too much social media).
- Pray that he would devote himself to the Scriptures.
- Pray that he would grow in his love for the Lord Jesus.
- Pray that he would grow in his love for the saints.
- Pray that he would grow in his ability to teach God's word.
- Pray that he would be kept from error.
- Pray that he would be faithful in evangelism.
- Pray that he would not give in to bitterness as he faces criticism.

- Pray for his refreshment when he is on vacation.
- Pray that he would delight in the Lord.

If your pastor is doing his job properly, he is praying for you, fighting for you. Paul describes his colleague Epaphras's praying for the Colossian believers as "struggling on your behalf in his prayers, that you may stand mature and fully assured in all the will of God" (Col. 4:12). What a great picture—pastor and people laboring, struggling, *fighting* in prayer for one another.

Do you pray for your pastor regularly? Daily? Specifically? Many of us, myself included, need to repent of the lip service we give to the idea that we pray for our pastors. Your pastor needs your earnest, prayerful support. Fight for him!

2

Encourage!

"Encourage one another and build one another up."

I THESSALONIANS 5:11

*"Most other people don't have criticism of
their job performance sent to their wife."*

AN ANONYMOUS PASTOR

COMPLAINING ABOUT LEADERS is not new. The people
of Israel consistently grumbled against Moses in the wilder-
ness (Ex. 15:24; 16:2; Num. 14:2; 16:3), to which the Lord
responded by putting some of them to death (1 Cor. 10:10).
God's response shows how spiritually dangerous it is to grumble
or complain against our leaders. Yet many of us, I imagine, do
not consider it a serious sin. When Paul is before the council in

Jerusalem on trumped-up charges, at one point he lets fly at one of his accusers who has just ordered him to be struck: "God is going to strike you, you whitewashed wall!" (Acts 23:3). The bystanders immediately tell Paul that he has insulted the high priest. Paul's response is fascinating. He doesn't retort with "Well, he deserves it—he was acting sinfully and has disgraced his office." Instead, he confesses his ignorance and wrongdoing: "I did not know, brothers, that he was the high priest, for it is written, 'You shall not speak evil of a ruler of your people'" (23:5, citing Ex. 22:28).

Our interactions with pastors probably never reach the level where we call them "whitewashed walls" or similar terms. However, these verses indicate the spiritual seriousness of speaking against our pastors. James reminds his readers, "Do not grumble against one another, brothers, so that you may not be judged; behold, the Judge is standing at the door" (James 5:9). Paul tells the Philippians to "do all things without grumbling or disputing, that you may be blameless and innocent, children of God without blemish in the midst of a crooked and twisted generation, among whom you shine as lights in the world" (Phil. 2:14–15). Biblically obedient Christians must *not* complain or grumble against their leaders.

I recently took part in a postsermon panel where people could text in questions to the pastor, who would then address them to members of the panel. The first question came from someone who asked why the panel was made up only of men. I sighed inwardly and thought, "That is your *first* comment? You have just heard a sermon and been given the chance to ask specific questions about application, you have the chance to think carefully about the implications of the sermon for your life, and the *first* thing you do is complain about the makeup of the panel?" But then I remembered that I also too often default to complaint rather than to encouragement.

A Pastor Writes:

Once one leader mentioned that he intentionally doesn't provide positive feedback or encouragement about my preaching ministry so that I don't get proud and sin. He also mentioned that as a leader, he saw his role as being the check and balance against the pastor. While every pastor needs accountability, that accountability cannot be divorced from encouragement or support. Without encouragement, it simply breeds distrust and fear. The best way to keep your pastor going for the long haul and not failing in ministry is not to watch him like a hawk but, instead, to encourage him in tangible and practical ways. Small, simple, and regular expressions of care and concern go much further than big gestures.

None of this rules out a place for raising concerns. Neither must we accept everything that a pastor does or says. In chapter 7, we will look at how to properly bring charges against a pastor, and in appendix 2, we will consider when and how to leave a church. However, in this chapter, while I acknowledge the danger of complaining, I want to concentrate on the positive counterpart—encouraging. If there is a place for giving careful, considered criticism to our pastors, normal church life should overflow with generous encouragement.

The root of this issue is that we often adopt a consumer mentality toward our pastors. We pay them and they serve us. So when they don't satisfy our wants in our time frame, we complain like we would in a restaurant if a meal were delivered slowly or not cooked well.

However, this is wrong on both fronts. My pastor is my leader, under God. My relationship to him is not the same as my relationship to my waiter in a restaurant (though I should also be considerate with my waiter). I give money to support the work of his ministry, but that does not make me his boss. I am also not passive—like a diner waiting to be served at a table. No, a better analogy is that the pastor is the headwaiter and I am also a waiter. All of us as Christians are meant to actively serve, which includes loving and encouraging other Christians, perhaps especially our pastors.

There are people in our churches who are cultural Christians, who are unconverted or have never matured despite years of church attendance. My guess is that if you are reading this book, you are more committed than most to supporting the ministry of your local church. Therefore, you can encourage your pastor by encouraging others to encourage him! And you can refuse to gossip and complain when others do it.

A Pastor Writes:

A specific word of encouragement or the opposite (particularly on Sundays) will linger long. General "thank-yous" are all very well, but specific encouragement (e.g., specific feedback on a sermon) is where the true building up occurs. It is not, I trust, mostly about ego. Most pastors genuinely want to know that the gifts they have been given by the Spirit are making a difference in building up others. It increases our worship. Discouragements in ministry easily feel like they outweigh encouragements. We don't want empty or shallow encouragement. However, even small thoughtful acts/words make a huge difference when we are counting our blessings before the Lord in prayer.

To say we should encourage our pastors seems banal. But to therefore write it off means we can easily forget to do it. And all too often we reduce encouragement to a quick "Thanks for the sermon, pastor" at the door. Paul reminds the Galatians that those who have been taught should "share all good things with the one who teaches" (Gal. 6:6). In its context, this command includes material support, but it also establishes a broader principle of supplying everything the pastor needs to keep going, and that includes encouragement.

Most of us are good at responsive encouragement. When our pastor preaches a particularly helpful sermon, we readily offer thanks. However, it is easy to adopt that consumer mentality I mentioned earlier, which causes us to express thanks or encouragement only when we receive benefit.

In order to encourage pastors more effectively, we need to adjust our thinking in three ways. First, we need to recognize that encouragement of others comes from a heart that is thankful to God. (The opposite is also true—a heart that defaults to complaint is one that is bitter toward God.) So the first step is to become better at thanking God. This is a neglected discipline among Christians. As a result, we often only pray *for* things rather than give thanks to God. But Paul tells the Thessalonians to "pray without ceasing" (1 Thess. 5:17) *and* to "give thanks in all circumstances," adding that "this is the will of God in Christ Jesus for you" (5:18). God wants us to give thanks to him. Cultivating a heart that is thankful to God will spill over to an attitude that is slow to criticize and quick to encourage others. You could start by writing down the things for which you are thankful. Perhaps you could incorporate that into your devotional time each day.

Second, encouragement of our pastor should be the overflow of a general life of encouragement. That is, while we should particularly encourage our pastor, he should not be the only object of our encouragement. Paul reflects on this dynamic in 1 Thessalonians: "Therefore *encourage one another* and *build one another up*, just as you are doing. We ask you, brothers, to respect those who labor among you and are over you in the Lord and admonish you, and to esteem them very highly in love because of their work. Be at peace among yourselves" (5:11–13). If believers should encourage one another, we must especially encourage our pastors.

But third, as we have just read, the pastor holds a particular place as one of those who "labor among you and are over you in the Lord and admonish you" (1 Thess. 5:12). God here commands us to "*respect*" our pastor and to "*esteem* [him] very highly in love because of [his] work" (5:12–13). Sometimes we think that people have to *earn* our respect and admiration. They have to prove themselves. God's economy differs: the pastor he has placed over us is, from the beginning, worthy of a respect and esteem that needs to translate into how we speak about and to him. We need to intentionally encourage him.

And so it is worth thinking of ways to encourage your pastor. He has a diverse job and probably does more than you know. (He does not work only on Sundays!) However, if you asked him, he would probably say that the *most* important thing that he does as a pastor is preach the word of God. Paul commanded Timothy to do this in the strongest way possible, charging him "in the presence of God and of Christ Jesus, who is to judge the living and the dead, and by his appearing and his kingdom" (2 Tim. 4:1). Your pastor carries many burdens, but this is the most public aspect of his job and the one about which he is probably most sensitive. It is also the aspect we find easiest to complain about ("My pastor is not as good a preacher as X"). So this is the area in which we can most powerfully encourage him.

Scripture lays the most serious charges on a pastor to preach faithfully. A pastor who is lazy in other areas can do damage, but a pastor who is lazy in the pulpit or does not preach faithfully can do untold eternal damage. So we have a responsibility to help him be a better preacher. *Sometimes* that may involve the well-chosen, prayed over, carefully thought about critique. *Much more often* it involves encouraging him in his preaching with *specific* feedback—not just "Thanks for the sermon today, pastor," but "Your application of verse 12 really hit home for me" or "I have never understood that passage before, but you explained it very clearly."

I know a number of pastors who find it difficult that communication with their people is often only one way. They preach, exhort, and encourage, but never receive any acknowledgment or indication that their labor is having any impact. It is easy to reply, "Well, that is his job—he gets paid to be a pastor," but like anyone, a pastor wants to know if he is doing a good job. He knows that ultimately he is accountable to God, but we can help him to execute his role faithfully, and we can do that by encouraging him.

Encouragement can also be more general. Paul uses the language of "comforting," which is related to encouragement. It is stronger than our idea of comfort, which often amounts to nothing more than patting someone on the back and uttering platitudes. It is actually a word that means to "strengthen." Paul uses it frequently in 2 Corinthians. He finishes the letter by telling them to "comfort one another" (2 Cor. 13:11). But he also reminds them that they comforted Titus, a Christian leader, when he came to them (7:7). Paul calls the Corinthians to be active in giving comfort—to one another, but also to Christian leaders.

A Pastor Writes:

Most people in a church don't realize that in general the ministry team only hears negative feedback. When things are going OK from a member's point of view, often people don't think to be encouraging. But when something doesn't please, the feedback comes quickly!

Your pastor is human. He will make mistakes. He will let you down. He will preach sermons that are not great. There will be periods when you will feel frustrated. What do you do in one of those periods? What if you are in one right now?

I have already mentioned the spiritual discipline of thankfulness—consciously, actively cultivating a heart of thankfulness. There is another spiritual discipline that we can adopt—complaining to God! It is fascinating how frequently in the psalms we read of the author complaining to God. For example, David writes, "Evening and morning and at noon / I utter my complaint and moan, / and he hears my voice" (Ps. 55:17). It is OK to lay out your struggles and complaints to God.

If you have valid concerns, it is also OK to discuss them with your pastor at the right time (not just after he has preached) and in the right way (after prayerfully examining your own heart). But it is not good to grumble or complain to your pastor.

Thoughtful, intentional encouragement of your pastor is a powerful way of loving him and helping him to persevere in his role. It should be the overflow of a thankful heart, saying to the pastor what we have been praying for him. It is also something that we as Christians are not very good at doing. We seem to be hardwired to complain, grumble, and criticize. It takes effort and conscious decision to deliberately and clearly encourage our pastor. Will you do it?

Listen!

"Why do you spend your money for that which is not bread,
and your labor for that which does not satisfy?
Listen diligently to me, and eat what is good,
and delight yourselves in rich food."

ISAIAH 55:2

"Most preachers know who the best listeners
are in sermons. They could name the handful
of people who week by week encourage them
merely by the way they listen. Conversely,
they also notice those on their phones, those
asleep, those unhappy with the preacher."

AN ANONYMOUS PASTOR

JESUS ADDRESSED A CROWD at one point and laid down a command and a principle: "Pay attention to what you hear: with the measure you use, it will be measured to you, and still more will be added to you" (Mark 4:24). He said this in the context of parables he had been teaching the crowd. Sometimes we think that Jesus spoke in parables, using the imagery of first-century Israel—soil, seeds, lights, bushels, and more—to make it *easier* for people to understand. But Mark says that Jesus told parables to keep people at a distance. They were like riddles—people could understand the surface meaning thanks to the earthy imagery, but only those (the disciples and others) who *approached* Jesus to ask for an explanation received "the secret of the kingdom," the true meaning of the parables (4:11). However, "for those outside everything is in parables, so that "'they may indeed see but not perceive, / and may indeed hear but not understand, / lest they should turn and be forgiven'"" (4:11–12, quoting Isa. 6:9–10). The principle is clear—those who actively listen, engage, and approach Jesus for explanation are rewarded with insight. Those who half-heartedly listen to what he says and then wander off are left outside. Therefore, we need to listen well—attentively and prayerfully—remembering that as our pastor preaches the word, it is the Lord who is speaking (1 Pet. 4:11).

A Pastor Writes:

In terms of church history, it is unlikely that this era will be known for its great reverence. We approach the Sunday gathering around the word of the Lord quite often with relative indifference. We don't necessarily come eagerly, grasping the awesome privilege with the expectation of hearing the Spirit speak to us as the word is prayerfully expounded.

Paul tells Timothy the role of the pastor is to "preach the word . . . in season and out of season; reprove, rebuke, and exhort, with complete patience and teaching" (2 Tim. 4:2). You can help your pastor fulfill this duty by being a good listener. That doesn't just mean staying awake and maintaining eye contact while he preaches (though that would certainly encourage him!); it means correctly receiving the word of God. After urging Timothy to preach the word, Paul immediately adds that "the time is coming when people will not endure sound teaching, but having itching ears they will accumulate for themselves teachers to suit their own passions" (4:3). Listening well to God's word means hearing it eagerly and letting it confront you—that is, allowing it to challenge and rebuke you. Listening badly means putting pressure on your pastor, whether indirectly (by lack of attention) or directly (by unfair criticism). This pressure can lead him—perhaps unconsciously—to preach to please his hearers.

If you humbly, submissively listen to the Scriptures, it will be easier for your pastor to preach the word. Scripture contains many passages and ideas that people in our generation don't like or actually hate—passages on the uniqueness of Christ or on gender and sex. A pastor who does his job will need to preach on such passages and topics. It will be easier for him if he knows that at least some people in the church are ready to submit to God's word and *listen* to it rather than simply expect God's word to affirm their preconceptions.

A pastor I know, a good and godly man, became so affected by his congregation (which contained a number of progressive and liberal Christians) that when he preached a sermon on a particularly confronting passage, he told his hearers, "I wish the Bible didn't say this." He went on to affirm the teaching of the passage, but he was revealing a heart under pressure. He knew what people in his congregation thought about that particular topic and was swaying to their opinions. As congregation members, we can strengthen our pastor by listening well and making sure we respond in a godly way to God's word.

A practical way to do this is to talk with one another after the service about the sermon. It is OK to talk about the weather, sports, politics, and other topics after worship, but it is sad that, at least in my experience, we so rarely talk about the sermon. But if our pastor sees us discussing his sermon and the passage he preached, he will be strengthened and encouraged to keep preaching and to take his preaching more seriously. If we never speak to one another—or to him—about his sermon, then we affirm by our behavior that we don't value his preaching.

A Pastor Writes:

I am genuinely not too worried if it was a "good" sermon that people enjoyed and found memorable, insightful, or even challenging. I want the word to dwell richly among the church community. I love it when, after the service, I hear the buzz of people talking about the implications of the passage. And then I love to see them actually do something about it.

But what do we do if our pastor is not a very good preacher? We can still do some practical things. Of course, we need to work even harder at listening. Perhaps we can do so with pen and paper in hand so that we can actively engage with the passage even if our pastor meanders or misses the point of the text. If he does not preach a great sermon, we can still encourage him afterward about the things he did well. We can also ask him about the passage and the parts we didn't understand because they weren't clearly explained. This can create a feedback loop. If the people who talk to the pastor about the sermon ask careful and thoughtful questions, they will encourage him to preach careful and thoughtful sermons.

There may be a place for a more pointed conversation with the pastor about his preaching. Remembering everything I said in the last chapter, and making sure we are not indulging a complaining or bitter spirit, it may be right for some people to sit down and help the pastor see how he could preach better sermons. For example, if he always preaches topical sermons, never getting into the riches of God's word as it is written, we could suggest an expository series. However, ideally this is the sort of thing that the elders in the church will bring up. Critically, this kind of feedback needs to be given in a humble, submissive, and noncomplaining way. If it is framed as coming from a hunger and an eagerness to hear the word every Sunday, a request for more of X, Y, and Z is more likely to be heard.

A Pastor Writes:

The purpose of the church is "to equip the saints for the work of ministry" (Eph. 4:12); therefore, the point of the sermon is not primarily to "inspire" or "refresh" in an interesting way that caters to everyone's various learning styles. Rather, it is to train and equip, and people should listen with that aim.

One reason we may find it hard to listen to our pastor is because we listen too much to the "great" preachers on the internet. I remember gushing to a famous preacher at a conference about how helpful I found his material. He thanked me and then pointedly reminded me that I should be expressing that kind of thanks to my own pastor. It was a helpful reminder. Our pastor—particularly if we attend a small church—often has less time than he would like to prepare his sermons. He deals with a lot of things his more famous counterparts delegate. He often feels that he could have done better with more time. But nearly always there is something helpful in his sermons, and we ought to listen to his preaching as eagerly as we listen to streamed sermons.

I preach occasionally and can think of one former congregation member who was particularly easy to preach to. He would sit forward, make eye contact, smile, and nod the whole way through the sermon—to look his way as I preached was a great encouragement. Another person would sit at the back and stifle yawns as I preached. The most discouraging moment came when I began my sermon and he left. I thought perhaps he was going to the restroom, but ten minutes later, he walked back in with a cup of coffee. It was hard not to feel deflated. I had been preaching my heart out while he got in line for coffee. The preacher notices that kind of thing.

A Pastor Writes:

When I last moved churches, I made a point of speaking to a handful of people who had been the best sermon listeners in my time in the church. I told them their active engagement, their note-taking, their nodding, their smiles, all these things had been encouraging for me as I preached week in and out. Most were shocked I'd even noticed and greatly encouraged to hear it, and I took the opportunity to encourage them to do it all the more.

Listening well is a spiritual discipline. We should go to church with an expectation that we will meet with God in the preaching of his word. All of us on occasion arrive tired and distracted, and when we are in that frame of mind, there is every chance the sermon will bounce off us. But if we are hungry, expectant, and ready to engage with God, then our experience will be much more positive. So we need to listen *actively*, not *passively*. It is easy to listen to a sermon without really hearing it. But it is better for us, and more encouraging for our pastor, if we engage carefully with the Scripture passage being taught and go away reflecting on both the passage and the sermon.

In addition to your pastor's sermons, you may be listening to others on the internet. But even if you don't listen to other sermons, it is hard to escape the proliferation of voices on social media. This chorus can sometimes be helpful, as it encourages thoughtful and reflective listening. However, it can create competing realms of authority. Rather than submitting ourselves to the preached word of God, we can easily find someone who simply endorses our opinions. There is a tension here. Of course our pastor is not always correct; of course we need to test everything he says against the word of God. But the default stance should be to listen and submit to what he says unless there is an obvious issue. We need to test all things, but we often apply this more stringently to our pastor than to our favorite internet preachers.

Of course, there is listening that *engages* and *understands*, but does not *obey*. We need to heed James's warning to "be doers of the word, and not hearers only" (James 1:22). There is real spiritual danger in loving good preaching for its own sake rather than as a means to meeting with the living God and responding to him with faith and repentance.

Your pastor is a flawed, fallible human being. But as he preaches the word of God, how you relate to what he says mirrors your relationship with God himself. Half-hearted listening to your pastor's preaching signifies a half-hearted Christian faith. Distracted listening suggests a distracted Christian faith. Refusal to obey the message preached points to a heart hardened against God and his gospel.

4

Give!

*"Each one must give as he has decided in his
heart, not reluctantly or under compulsion,
for God loves a cheerful giver."*

2 CORINTHIANS 9:7

*"I wish people understood that giving
is about having a heart of worship. I'm
not just singing for my supper."*

AN ANONYMOUS PASTOR

THE NEW TESTAMENT commands that a pastor be paid. Paul teaches it in 1 Corinthians: "Do you not know that those who are employed in the temple service get their food from the temple, and those who serve at the altar share in the sacrificial offerings? In the same way, the Lord commanded that those who proclaim the gospel should get their living by the gospel" (1 Cor. 9:13–14). Although Paul has laid aside this "right" (9:15), the principle enunciated here and elsewhere (Gal. 6:6; 1 Tim. 5:17–18) is that a congregation should pay its pastor.

Some churches, though, make life unnecessarily hard for their pastor and his family. I heard of a church where the elders met to discuss the pastor's salary. They brought him into the room to discuss his pay. After the meeting, one of the elders told him that if he had pushed harder, they would have happily given him more. This is the wrong way around. A congregation should be as generous as it can be with its pastor. Let him give back to the church if he thinks he is paid too much.

Some pastors are paid too much. There is an Instagram account called PreachersNSneakers that calls out pastors who have excessively expensive sneakers. I am not sure how helpful this kind of social media activism is, but the point is well made—some pastors are getting rich at the expense of the people of God. However, if you are reading this book, you probably don't go to a church where your pastor wears Yeezy sneakers. Your pastor more likely has the opposite problem.

I spent some time on the mission field, where I saw pastors in both situations. Some lived in poverty out of necessity. Their congregations did not have the means to support them

A Pastor Writes:

Pastors are often nervous when it comes to giving. We fear people think it is about our pay. Not many people have their income put on a spreadsheet each year for the congregation to see and judge if he is worth it! At our annual members' meeting last year, one dear brother noted that I had not had an in-line-with-inflation pay increase for nearly three years. He not only raised it publicly but suggested that seeing as there had been a three-year gap, it ought to be slightly above the inflationary index.

adequately. But I also saw the opposite—pastors and churches that received big donations from Western churches, with the result that the lifestyle of the pastor did not align with that of the congregation. This disparity was deeply unhelpful.

The Bible encourages generosity—for the sake of our pastors, as well as for the ministry as a whole. Congregation members should be as generous as possible and trust that the pastor will, in turn, be as generous as he can. I know of churches that saw a dip in giving when their pastors moved on because those men were giving significant amounts back to the churches they served.

A Pastor Writes:

I went five years without any review of my pay. I then felt I needed to say something. They were surprised that I was disappointed to be offered just 1 percent more after the five years. It felt like there was no commitment to keep my salary in line with inflation.

Paul twice quotes Deuteronomy 25:4, which says, "You shall not muzzle an ox when it is treading out the grain." In the first of Paul's quotations, in 1 Corinthians 9:9, he immediately insists that God's primary concern is not for cattle but for human workers and their congregations. He then asks "If we have sown spiritual things among you, is it too much if we reap material things from you?" (9:11). This is quite confronting: a minister should "reap" material benefit from those whom he serves. Even though Paul puts aside what he describes as his "rightful claim" (9:12) or his "rights" (9:15), the principle he lays down holds. God commands that pastors be paid—just as temple workers in the Old Testament were to be paid (9:13). But how much? The New Testament does not lay down a pay scale. But it does speak about generosity. It is surely right that those of us who can influence a pastor's compensation be motivated by generosity.

In fact, the second place where Paul quotes Deuteronomy 25:4 points in the same direction. In 1 Timothy 5:18, Paul cites the verse and then applies it with the words of Jesus: "The laborer deserves his wages" (Luke 10:7). This provides biblical precedent for the principle already laid down in 1 Timothy 5:17: "Let the elders who rule well be considered worthy of double honor, especially those who labor in preaching and teaching." What does Paul mean by "double honor"? The word translated as "honor" is the same word for a price or the value for something. So it is possible to take this verse in a more economic direction. Commentators disagree on precisely what is meant here by "double." It could mean "ample," which is how the word is translated in the Holman Christian Standard Bible: "The elders who are good leaders should be considered worthy of an ample honorarium, especially those who work hard at preaching and teaching." Or it could mean double in the sense that if elders work a secular job, it is still right that they should be paid for their pastoral work (i.e., "double" refers to their secular pay and pastoral pay). Also, it could be that Paul is playing on the word "honor," which can mean both pay and respect, and is saying that elders should receive both. In any case, the principle of generosity toward a pastor is underlined.

We have to be careful in projecting our twenty-first-century situation back onto the text of the New Testament. It is unlikely that there were full-time paid pastors of the kind we are used to until the second century, and so we can't press 1 Timothy 5:17 too hard as a "law" for how we are to treat our pastors. However, it is Paul's general principle for which I am arguing—that we should be as generous as we can to our pastors.

Of course, if our church is small and the congregation earns little, we won't be able to give as much to our pastor as another church might. He may have to work another job to support himself and his family. But the principle of generosity, of willingness to give what we can, still stands. What is deeply troubling—something I have seen all too often—is a wealthy congregation that pays the pastor peanuts.

People offer some unhelpful reasons for not generously supporting their pastor. Some believe that a pastor—following the Lord Jesus—should be poor. Ironically, the people making this argument are often very wealthy. I have heard of church treasurers taking almost vindictive pleasure in ensuring that their pastors are not paid too much while they themselves are living lavish lifestyles. We can mistakenly think that the money we give to our pastor is *our* money, that *we* earned it. However, God's word asks us, "What do you have that you did not receive?" (1 Cor. 4:7). The Lord has given

A Pastor Writes:

Our children were quizzed on how much allowance they received and what sorts of holiday activities they were allowed to do. The other church children felt it was important to work out how the ministry family spent its money, given that "our parents pay your parents, so my Mum and Dad are actually paying your pocket money and for your movie outings." The other church children thought it was hilarious. Our children were mortified.

you whatever wealth you have, and he expects you to show a corresponding generosity toward all people, especially your pastor. In Paul's words, the rich are "to be generous and ready to share" (1 Tim. 6:18).

Sometimes, if the pastor's wife works, church members believe they are relieved of their obligation to pay him. But the principle laid down in both 1 Corinthians 9 and 1 Timothy 5 remains—a pastor (like any worker) should be paid for the work he does. The pastor and his family may, in turn, decide to give back to the church.

None of this denies that some pastors abuse their position to fleece their flocks. Often they are high-profile pastors, so we latch on to the excesses of the worst-case scenario. But the pastors I know more often worry about their own financial situations and the viability of their churches.

It is also important to note that giving is about more than the pastor's pay—it shapes the general church budget. If the congregation does not give, then the pastor will struggle to maintain the church's ministries. So our generosity goes beyond the pastor's lifestyle or ability to support his family. It enables the wider ministry of the church.

A Pastor Writes:

There is little that is more difficult for a pastor than raising the issue of a church member and giving. Genuinely, I am more comfortable with people confessing sexual sin or some other aspect of church discipline. We need to talk about money—Jesus warns about it so much—but it is tough. Asking me about it really helps break the ice and get the conversation going.

Second Corinthians 9 is another chapter about giving, but not giving within the church. Paul is calling for Gentile Christians to support Jewish Christians in Jerusalem. Nevertheless,

Paul lays down principles of generosity that relate to our own situation. In each of our chapters, we have seen that our behavior flows from our relationship with the Lord: if we are thankful to him, we will be thankful and encouraging toward our pastor. In this chapter, we see that trusting the Lord frees us from the fear of being generous. Specifically, Paul writes, "Whoever sows sparingly will also reap sparingly, and whoever sows bountifully will also reap bountifully" (2 Cor. 9:6). This is not the prosperity gospel by the backdoor. This is a principle that runs throughout Scripture: if you are lavishly generous, you will reap spiritually in that you will have the joy of seeing the ministry you support flourish. That's how Paul expands this teaching later: "He who supplies seed to the sower and bread for food will supply and multiply your seed for sowing and increase the harvest of your righteousness" (9:10).

As well as calling for generosity, Paul lays down the principle that giving should be willing and cheerful: "Each one must give as he has decided in his heart, not reluctantly or under compulsion, for God loves a cheerful giver" (2 Cor. 9:7). However much we give, we should give from the heart, not under a sense of obligation and not reluctantly. A church of healthy, generous givers will not have to worry about finances because it is a church that trusts the Lord.

Forgive!

"Be kind to one another, tenderhearted, forgiving one another, as God in Christ forgave you."

EPHESIANS 4:32

"I recently got a terrible telling off from someone who claimed that I did not care for the church as much as the last pastor did. This centered around the fact that I had missed reading something in a WhatsApp group. What people don't realize is that as the pastor you can be added to lots of these groups, and it is time-consuming to respond to each one."

AN ANONYMOUS PASTOR

YOUR PASTOR IS a sinful human being. He will fail. He will let you down. What will you do when he does?

Sometimes pastoral failings are extremely serious (sins such as adultery, abuse, or criminal activity). Those kinds of behavior (which we will talk about in chap. 7) are at one end of the spectrum. At the other end are situations in which we saddle our pastor with unreasonable expectations. Here the problem is with us, not with our pastor. It has been a week and he has not visited me. It has been an hour and he has not responded to my message. I made a suggestion that has not been implemented. He thanked another member but not me.

However, between these extremes of our unreasonable expectations and his major sins are the kinds of failings and minor sins that require no formal action, just the understanding and forgiveness that ought to mark every Christian relationship.

So what should you do if your pastor has hurt you? First of all, recognize his failings. All of us have failings that our friends and families live with.

I attended a church during my university years with a pastor who, under God, I think saved me from drifting off into a very unhelpful form of Christianity. I had been through a number of churches where I was chasing experience. When I arrived at this church, I found a ministry built on the solid

A Pastor Writes:

Pastoral ministry is relationally tiring. With all the relationships that exist in a church, there are many opportunities for misunderstanding and even open conflict. And then the minister is often expected to "sort it out." These things keep us awake at night and take a toll on family life more than anything else. Nobody ever gets it 100 percent right, and the bruising it causes can accumulate over time.

meat of good expository preaching, something I had never experienced before.

However, my pastor had a failing—he had a terrible memory. I don't just mean that he occasionally forgot where he left his keys—his memory issues were on a totally different level. In the days before cell phones, his wife needed to leave an alarm clock on with a note under it to remind him to go to the dentist. He once had to fill up his car with gas, but when he arrived at the gas station near his house, he realized he had walked there! Another time he remembered to drive there, but when he arrived home, he realized that he had walked home and had left his two sons in the car at the gas station!

This inability to remember things did not combine well with another of his positive characteristics—a strong commitment to welcome newcomers to our church. Stories abounded of him welcoming people as visitors after they had been coming to our church for weeks. One of my friends took umbrage when the pastor greeted him for the third week running, saying, "Hello! Are you new?" My friend replied, "No! I am not! This is the third time we have met in as many weeks. I won't be coming to this church anymore!"

My friend's reaction was neither loving nor gracious. He had an opportunity for "bearing with one another and . . . forgiving each other" (Col. 3:13). Forgiveness does not always have to be formal. Peter tells his readers to "keep loving one another earnestly, since love covers a multitude of sins" (1 Pet. 4:8). He is not giving a theology of atonement. His point is that human relationships need this kind of forgiveness to survive. This forgiveness means we do not *always* have to confront others and call them to repentance for *every* wrong they do to us. There are times when we should not even mention a wrong done to us, but simply overlook it.

Proverbs reminds us that "good sense makes one slow to anger, / and it is his glory to overlook an offense" (19:11). As evangelicals, we take sins seriously, know that repentance is critical, and understand that Jesus had to die for our sins.

A Pastor Writes:

A family was threatening to leave church. The members of the family felt unloved. After a conversation, it became clear that what they meant was "The pastor isn't our best friend." Lots of people in church were loving them, but because the pastor only occasionally had them over socially, they felt neglected. Sadly, even when it was pointed out that the pastor can't possibly be everyone's best friend and that the church as a body was doing very well, it was still not enough.

But there is a place for overlooking and not confronting every sin. Every good marriage operates on that principle, as does any healthy friendship, including our relationship with our pastor. Your pastor might make mistakes and let you down. God's word shows you that the best way to deal with some of those mistakes and failings is to simply overlook them.

Paul talks about relational breakdown between Christians in the Corinthian church. People are actually taking their Christian brothers and sisters to court, and Paul is appalled. It is a bad witness before unbelievers (1 Cor. 6:6) and a failure to realize that the church should be equipped to solve such problems (6:2–3). Paul lays down a principle that will help all of us relate to other Christians—including our pastor: "Why not rather suffer wrong?" (6:7). This is Paul's application of Jesus's command to turn the other cheek (Matt. 5:39). He is not talking about a crime or a serious sin, but he is speaking of a matter that is serious enough to be taken to court. And yet, Paul and Jesus speak of letting go of formal justice, of bearing the wrong, of overlooking the offense by turning our cheek and moving on.

Our world does not model this. If you have spent any time on Twitter, you know that people are slow to overlook offenses. We as Christians should be different, and we can start in our relationship with our pastor.

But what about when your pastor hurts you deeply or does something that, although it does not call his ministry into question, nevertheless compels you to say something?

First of all, examine your own heart. You may be over-reacting. It is possible that what the pastor did or said was really not that significant—even if it hurt at the time. Years ago, my pastor snapped at me as I tried to chat with him at an outreach event. It stung a little and it wasn't right, but he was under a lot of pressure organizing everything. I had two options—have a brief chat with him later and tell him that his words hurt me or just overlook them. I did the latter. (If it had happened a second time, I would have had a chat with him.)

It is also worth letting a little time pass before you bring a matter up with your pastor. The intensity of the hurt may fade a little with time, and you may then decide that you can and should overlook the matter. However, if you still feel that you should say something, communicating clearly, gently, and fairly with your pastor may be the best option.

A Pastor Writes:

One dear sister had some complaints about how she had been supported pastorally. She carefully and prayerfully considered them, wrote them out by hand, and asked to come and see me and my wife together. She was clear, robust, gracious. Not all of it was accurate—but she never claimed it was. It did lead to forgiveness, action, and better pastoring of others.

The pressures of the job mean that our pastor—who is human—sometimes behaves less than perfectly. The choice we face is to gossip or complain (which are ruled out by Scripture), to lovingly speak with our pastor (which can help in certain circumstances), or to lovingly overlook the offense (which is often the best course of action).

Submit!

*"Obey your leaders and submit to them, for
they are keeping watch over your souls, as those
who will have to give an account. Let them
do this with joy and not with groaning, for
that would be of no advantage to you."*

HEBREWS 13:17

*"I think the hardest thing as a pastor today is the
rising tide of consumerism. The bar is continually
set higher to deliver more than the time before.
You clear it ninety-nine times as it gets higher
and higher, but then bomb the hundredth."*

AN ANONYMOUS PASTOR

SUBMISSION IS perhaps the most unpopular teaching in the Bible. Often this is because people misunderstand submission, thinking the Bible requires unquestioning obedience—a recipe for abuse and terrible sin. This is not the place to address all of the broader issues associated with submission, except to say that, whether in marriage or any other relationship, the Bible does not teach unquestioning obedience and does not promote abuse.

Even those who know and love the Bible, however, can feel the world's hostility to submission and are understandably nervous because of the way people have twisted it. We also might find ourselves reacting to the word or the principle when we hear it mentioned.

Yet the New Testament is clear—there is a right and proper submission to those who are in spiritual leadership over us. Paul tells the Corinthians to be subject or to submit to "every fellow worker and laborer" (1 Cor. 16:16). Peter tells those who are younger to "be subject to the elders" (1 Pet. 5:5). Hebrews widens it to every Christian, commanding them to "obey your leaders and submit to them" (Heb. 13:17).

What does submission to our leaders actually mean? It is easy to say what it doesn't mean. It doesn't mean that we have to do everything they tell us. It doesn't mean that they have a say over every area of our lives. Sadly, there are too many

A Pastor Writes:

The onus is on the congregation to submit to the one in authority and make it a joy to lead the congregation. It is not the reverse. Currently the mood is that it is the responsibility of the senior minister to make it a joy for people to come to church, to fulfill them, to please their children, to keep things interesting, to cater to everyone, to submit to their wishes, and to consider their enjoyment at all times.

examples of what is euphemistically called "heavy shepherding." I know of churches where members must show their bank accounts to the leaders so that they can determine whether the members are giving enough. I know a church where members have to clear their vacation plans with the elders. There have been churches where college students were told not to go home for the holidays since the church should be their primary family. This distorts what the Bible means by submission.

Submission in human relationships never means absolute obedience. Paul actually criticizes believers in the Corinthian church for allowing themselves to be badly treated by false teachers: "You bear it if someone makes slaves of you, or devours you, or takes advantage of you, or puts on airs, or strikes you in the face" (2 Cor. 11:20). This important verse is often overlooked. Wrong submission to the wrong people is inappropriate and can lead to brutality. Paul utterly rejected abusive "leadership," and so should we. Submission does not mean allowing ourselves to be mistreated.

However, the challenge comes when we are asked to do something right and appropriate, but we don't want to do it. We readily submit when asked to do something we're glad to do, but it becomes much harder when it is something we don't want to do. For instance, I might not like paying taxes or obeying certain laws, but the apostles teach that I must submit to government authorities (Rom. 13:1; Titus 3:1; 1 Pet. 2:13–14). Again, this is never an absolute submission, a requirement to do something that is contrary to God's word. Nevertheless, I am called to submit whether I like it or not.

The problem often arises when we think of submission not in biblical but in secular terms. Parallels from business or sports can be helpful, but they too easily distort the picture. A pastor is not a CEO, coach, or captain. The Bible puts submission in marriage and the church primarily in the framework of *love*. Within a biblical marriage, a wife submits to a husband who reflects Christ, the Lord who laid down his life for the

A Pastor Writes:

A person suddenly announced a decision to leave the church. I was shocked and said, "Let's talk about this as mature Christians." The person's response was to the effect, "I pay you to serve me. Your role is not to question me." This is a very sad picture of how someone might understand God's word on how churches work.

church (Eph. 5:24–25).[1] Similarly, in Paul's relationship with the Corinthian Christians, he expects them to repent and to submit to him (as Christ's apostle). Nevertheless, he can also say, "What we proclaim is not ourselves, but Jesus Christ as Lord, with ourselves as your servants for Jesus' sake" (2 Cor. 4:5). Especially in 2 Corinthians we get a picture of a man who deeply loves this church: "We have spoken freely to you, Corinthians; our heart is wide open. You are not restricted by us, but you are restricted in your own affections" (6:11–12). Paul adds, "You are in our hearts, to die together and to live together" (7:3).

---

1   I have been greatly helped to understand what biblical submission is and is not by my friend and colleague Lionel Windsor.

A Pastor Writes:

The pastor isn't the "hired help"—he is freed up from secular work so he can be the leader (first among equals), but he is not solely responsible for the work of Christ's body the church because "It's his job." We are all responsible—so maybe take a moment and see if you can suggest a solution to the issue that you are part of rather than just drop another problem onto his to-do list!

Submission has three elements. First, it relates to the Scriptures. Believers practice submission and obedience to leaders primarily as those leaders function as teachers of God's word. Since Paul tells Timothy to "preach the word; be ready in season and out of season; reprove, rebuke, and exhort, with complete patience and teaching" (2 Tim. 4:2), then submission means allowing yourself to be reproved, rebuked, and exhorted. It means allowing your pastor to point out where you are being inconsistent in your Christian faith. Of course, we don't like to be rebuked. But Scripture instructs the pastor to rebuke in some cases (Titus 1:9, 13). In fact, Paul tells Titus to "exhort and rebuke with all authority. Let no one disregard you" (2:15). When was the last time your pastor rebuked you? Maybe he never has. How would you react if he did?

Second, submission relates to humility. When Peter speaks of submission, he expands on it in terms of humility: "Likewise, you who are younger, be subject to the elders. Clothe yourselves, all of you, with humility toward one another, for 'God opposes the proud but gives grace to the humble'" (1 Pet. 5:5). Submission is a recognition that we need to be led, that we have leaders, and that while we enjoy equal standing before God with those leaders, we have different roles within the church. God appoints people who make decisions affecting the church and calls us to be subject to them.

Third, submission relates to the life of the church. This is a more general submission. The pastor decides to change the morning service from 10:30 to 9:30. What do you do? The pastor decides to shorten the youth group meeting by half an hour and give it a clearer Bible focus. What do you do? These are the sorts of things we find challenging. There is no right or wrong time to start a service and no right or wrong length of time for a youth fellowship. When we have strong opinions, it can be hard for us to submit. But this is precisely where we need to yield our authority.

Submission is a matter of the heart as we willingly yield to another person. We will sometimes struggle with decisions taken by our leaders, but we must submit. The fact that this makes us uncomfortable—perhaps especially in a Western context—shows us how our own thinking is shaped by Western individualism rather than the Bible. We may resist any kind of submission because of extreme cases of abuse—of a pastor calling for us to do something immoral or hurtful—but we have seen that the New Testament actively condemns that kind of submission.

Submission may be the most countercultural thing that we can do. But the Bible commands it, our church's health requires it, and our identity in Christ must reflect it. Furthermore, it is a wonderful way to show love to our pastors. The better we respond to our faithful leaders, the better it will be for both us and them. As the author to the Hebrews says after telling his readers to obey and submit to their leaders, "Let them do this with joy and not with groaning, for that would be of no advantage to you" (Heb. 13:17). You can bless your pastor (and yourself) by your godly submission.

Check!

*"Do not admit a charge against an elder except
on the evidence of two or three witnesses."*

I TIMOTHY 5:19

*"I was accused of spiritual abuse, investigated
by the church leadership, acquitted, and then
acquitted a second time when the complainants
appealed the decision and it was reviewed by a
third-party organization. But the truth of the
allegations don't ever really matter, the fact of
the allegations is all some people need for trust
to be broken and suspicion to be sown."*

AN ANONYMOUS PASTOR

WHAT SHOULD WE DO when our pastor is accused of serious sins?

In this chapter, we will consider how to support our pastors in a very different way. The sad fact is that some pastors are accused of serious sins. As well as praying for them, we also need to support our pastors by ensuring, as much as it depends on us, that the accusations are dealt with in a transparent, biblical way.

I'm not speaking here of criminal behavior (such as domestic violence, sexual abuse, and similar sins), which must be dealt with by the appropriate authorities. If you suspect or receive information that your pastor is engaging in criminal activity, then you need to inform the police and denominational authorities immediately. Sadly, too many people have been hurt because Christians have tried to deal with matters like these "in-house." Turning to the police in these situations does not violate 1 Corinthians 6, which concerns not *criminal* matters but what we might term *civil* matters, such as lawsuits.

This chapter will consider what we can call, for want of a better term, "major" sins. These are the sorts of sins that disqualify a pastor from the ministry—such sins as adultery or alcohol addiction. We will concentrate on one sin in particular: spiritual abuse or bullying. Although Scripture never uses this specific language, the Lord condemns evil shepherds who destroy the flock (Jer. 23:1–2). Likewise, Peter warns that a pastor must not be "domineering over those in [his] charge" (1 Pet. 5:3). We saw in the last chapter that Paul rebuked the Corinthian Christians for enduring false teachers who treated the church harshly: "You bear it if someone makes slaves of you, or devours you, or takes advantage of you, or puts on airs, or strikes you in the face" (2 Cor. 11:20). The Bible describes these types of leaders as wolves disguised as sheep (Matt. 7:15). As Paul puts it, just as "Satan disguises himself as an angel of light . . . it is no surprise if his servants, also, disguise themselves as servants of righteousness" (2 Cor. 11:14–15).

As I write this, the evangelical world continues to reel from multiple spiritual abuse scandals. High-profile pastors and evangelists have been exposed for their abusive behavior. Sadly, this is not new. For too long, evangelicals have overlooked and excused abusive behavior so that high-profile successful Christian leaders were able to continue their destructive ministries. Now, it seems, we are much more vigilant—and that is a good thing. The New Testament clearly teaches that pastors can and do fall. Some of the harshest condemnation in Scripture is for leaders who abuse their positions and inflict pain on the flock. That is true in both the Old and New Testaments. However, the Scriptures are equally clear that when a leader is accused, there needs to be a process. There is a danger that in our eagerness to pass judgment, the proper process will be short-circuited, and pastors will be caught up in the collateral damage.

A Pastor Writes:

When I was accused, my wife and I knew how false every facet of the accusation was. I know I am a sinner, but the details and extent of the accusations were so far from the truth that you would think I could take comfort in that. Instead, it seemed as if I had the words of the accusation running on replay in my head every moment of every day. It took nine months for resolution and the truth to be revealed and for me to be cleared. During those months, I fell into depression, bouts of heightened anxiety, and panic attacks that almost crippled my ministry and me as a person. These false accusations disoriented me, ate at me; I resonated with Paul, who writes that he "despaired of life itself" (2 Cor. 1:8). Had I not remembered that Jesus himself was falsely accused, and been supported by my wife, elders, and dear friends, I don't know how I would have survived this.

In one sense, this chapter might be the one that you as a reader will be least able to directly apply. Accusations of this nature should be dealt with at an elder or denominational level. However, as congregation members, it is important to understand the principles laid down by Scripture so that if we or others have been bullied or spiritually abused, we know what should and should not happen.

Paul articulates the process that should be followed when an elder or pastor has been accused of a significant sin: "Don't accept an accusation against an elder unless it is supported by two or three witnesses. Publicly rebuke those who sin, so that the rest will be afraid" (1 Tim. 5:19–20 CSB).

What does Paul mean by "accept an accusation"? The language points to a formal reception of an accusation. Paul envisages a structure in which a person or body can receive accusations made against an elder.

What kind of accusations are in view? The word translated as "accusation," rare in the New Testament, indicates anything that might bring the pastor into public disrepute. In listing the qualifications of an elder, Paul writes that he must be "above reproach" (1 Tim. 3:2; Titus 1:6–7). So this kind of accusation, if proven, would mean that the pastor is no longer above reproach. The accusations in view here, then, could include those sins (marital unfaithfulness, not managing a household well, and so on) that, if proven true, would make a pastor's position untenable. However, Paul says the response to a charge being upheld is a public rebuke (1 Tim. 5:20). This may mean that the sin in question, while serious enough to merit public rebuke, is not serious enough to merit being removed from the ministry.[1]

What does Paul mean by "two or three witnesses"? Does he mean that at least two people have to catch the pastor in

A Pastor Writes:

On one occasion, I was emailed by a church member claiming that she was furious with me about things she "had heard about me." However, she refused to tell me what she had heard. She also refused to meet to explain even after I asked if I had done anything that required forgiveness. I still do not know precisely why she was so angry and have had to piece the false accusations together from family members and friends. She has subsequently left our church.

---

1   I think the CSB is more accurate than the ESV at this point. The ESV implies unrepentant sin ("As for those who persist in sin, rebuke them in the presence of all"), which is a possible reading, but I think the CSB fits the overall context better: "Publicly rebuke those who sin."

the sin before an accusation can be lodged? "Two or three witnesses" comes from the Old Testament. An Israelite who committed a capital offense (e.g., engaging in idol worship) was to be executed only "on the evidence of two witnesses or of three witnesses" (Deut. 17:6) and after those investigating had "inquire[d] diligently" that it was "true and certain" that the sin had been committed (17:4). So Moses rules out the death penalty on the basis of the testimony of just one witness. In Deuteronomy 19, Moses deals with lesser offenses, but the same principle of two or three witnesses applies. He explicitly states that "a single witness shall not suffice against a person for any crime or for any wrong in connection with any offense that he has committed. Only on the evidence of two witnesses or of three witnesses shall a charge be established" (19:15). In this passage, Moses also raises the possibility of a "malicious witness" who falsely accuses someone (19:16). Again, those who investigate are to "inquire diligently" (19:18), and if the testimony proves to be untrue, the false witness is to receive the punishment for the crime concerning which he made the false accusation (19:19).

Not all of what Moses says in Deuteronomy carries over into the life of the church. For example, Paul does not confer upon the church the authority to put people to death. However, we should note the following. First, it is not that *only* elders or pastors should be judged on the basis of two or three witnesses, while everyone else can be accused on the basis of one witness. Nevertheless, Paul understands that pastors, due to the public nature of their role, are particularly liable to accusation and wants to remind Timothy that due process needs to be followed. But how strictly should we apply the "two or three witnesses" standard? Are the witnesses "eyewitnesses"? Sadly, people have used this uncertainty to attempt to hide their sins. However, a moment's reflection shows that "eyewitnesses" would be an incredibly restrictive requirement. It would mean, for example, that a pastor who embezzled the church's giving could not be held to account unless two or three people actually *saw* him transferring the money. No, Paul is not laying down such a tight requirement.

When Jesus applies the principle of "two or three witnesses" in Matthew 18, the offended person is simply told to "take one or two others along with you"—that is, people to whom the offended person has explained what has happened. In other words, Jesus envisages a situation in which there might be no direct *eyewitnesses* to the offense of the accused against the accuser, yet he still teaches that the accusation can be established in the presence of witnesses. He is saying that no one should be condemned on the basis of a single accusation, with no evidence; but neither is he saying that a person can't bring an accusation unless he has two or three eyewitnesses to the sin. An individual can bring an accusation, but the facts have to be established in the presence of witnesses. Part of establishing the facts may involve corroborative evidence (which might serve as the two or three witnesses that Deuteronomy speaks about). In other words, "there may not always be 2–3 eyewitnesses—but there may be corroborative evidence; there may be texts, emails, documents, minutes, patterns of conduct seen over a period of time by multiple witnesses that corroborate the testimony of a single victim or abused person."[2]

Following investigation by the denomination, other elders, or a third-party organization (1 Tim. 5:19–20 would allow for any of these options), the church leadership should "publicly rebuke those who sin, so that the rest will be afraid" (1 Tim. 5:20 CSB). "Those who sin" could be the accused elder or (echoing what we saw in Deuteronomy 19) those bringing a malicious charge. Of course, the charge might be proved wrong and the person bringing it might be found not to have brought it maliciously, in which case no rebuke would be necessary.[3] Paul is envisaging a public resolution to the issue.

---

2 Jonathan Gibson, "Orthopraxy: The Life of the Minister in the Life of His Ministry" (unpublished manuscript). I am thankful to Jonny for his input on this whole section.
3 Gibson's book will explore this possibility further.

Because of the potential for serious ministerial falls, those who ordain people to the eldership should do so cautiously. They are not to "be hasty in the laying on of hands," because to do so would be to "take part in the sins of others" (1 Tim. 5:22) when they fall.

Paul finishes this section of his letter to Timothy by affirming that whether or not sins come to light in this life, they will not escape God's judgment (1 Tim. 5:24). Likewise, good deeds done by a minister, whether seen by people in this life or not, will one day be revealed (5:25). Paul seems to widen the discussion at this point, but the principle he lays down applies to what he said earlier about charges against an elder: the truth will come out.

A Pastor Writes:

A family left our church a few years ago. To this day, we hear of conversations in which someone from those people's new church says, "Did you hear what their last pastor and his wife did to them?" This is painful beyond what we can bear sometimes, especially because we know what really happened but can't tell anyone. It's almost unbearable to live with lies laid against you for a long time, if not a lifetime.

In a fallen world, sadly, things often will go wrong in the relationship between pastor and congregation. We touched on this in chapter 5, where we saw the need to forgive a pastor's failings. In this chapter, we are talking about situations where the stakes are much higher, so these matters must be dealt with carefully, publicly, and justly.

If the tendency in the past was to automatically believe the pastor and sideline the victim (often with devastating consequences), the danger now is that we *over*correct and believe the pastor is guilty by default. Both extremes are pastorally disastrous. Victims must be cared for, but laying charges against a pastor is a serious matter and is not to be done lightly. The matter must be investigated. The guilty pastor must be rebuked and possibly removed if found to be not above reproach. The innocent pastor must be exonerated before those who know that charges have been brought. If the charges are deemed malicious (rather than innocently mistaken), those bringing them must be rebuked.

As members of a church, when a complaint against the pastor arises, we may not (and probably should not) know all the details. As difficult as it may be, we need to reserve judgment. This means we should relate to any complainants as if they are telling the truth *and* relate to the pastor as if he is innocent. The inclination today toward an unbiblical understanding of

> **A Pastor Writes:**
>
> Problems are best dealt with face to face and swiftly. All too often church members allow tension to build over months and months, and then unleash false accusations in a verbal volley through their fingers online. I want people to come and talk, and feel free to do so. I also want them to know that these are the sort of things that destroy a pastor's sleep, can be destructive in his marriage and family life, and make him question being in pastoral ministry.

power dynamics (anyone with power is *automatically* more suspect) means that the default is to favor the complainant. However, we cannot prejudge a case, but must love and support both parties until the matter is resolved.

It is no small thing for a victim to make a charge that is dismissed, not handled properly, or not resolved justly. Victims have been left broken when the wrong done to them was not properly acknowledged and the perpetrators allowed to escape any censure. They lose sleep, they develop illnesses, and their families suffer.

It is also no small thing for a pastor to have a charge laid against him that is false, not handled properly, or not resolved justly. Pastors have been left broken by false accusations that were not exposed or properly resolved. They lose sleep, they develop illnesses, and their families suffer.

Nothing I have written is meant to minimize the real pain that people have suffered from abusive pastors. This chapter is not an argument to go easy on pastors or withhold accusations. It is an appeal, however, that these matters must be handled biblically (through a careful investigation with due process and a just verdict reached on the basis of the evidence, established in the presence of two or three witnesses). Failure to do so can result in terrible damage to the complainant, the accused, and the wider church.

The stakes are very high, and until such a matter is resolved one way or another, the complainant and the accused both need a lot of care and support, as they will when the process has concluded. Such cases present an opportunity for the evil one to ruin lives, and they require much prayer, humility, and trust in God on the part of church members.

Conclusion

*"Pay careful attention to yourselves and to all
the flock, in which the Holy Spirit has made
you overseers, to care for the church of God,
which he obtained with his own blood."*

ACTS 20:28

*"The majority of feedback the minister gets is
silence or negative. Don't assume other people
are saying thank you, they really aren't."*

AN ANONYMOUS PASTOR

EVERY CHRISTIAN IS CALLED by the Lord Jesus to carry
his or her cross and follow him (Mark 8:34). Every Christian
lives with the opposition of the flesh, the world, and the devil.
The New Testament constantly urges Christians not to give
up, to keep trusting Jesus, to keep living for him.

In his kindness, God has given us pastors to teach us God's word, to rebuke us, and to encourage us. Your pastor has the most rewarding job—serving the Lord Jesus by leading God's people by teaching them God's word. Your pastor also has the most challenging job, because so often the opposition that the devil aims at the church is focused on the pastor. If a pastor stops preaching the truth or stops calling for genuine repentance, the devil wins.

High-profile failures of pastors have been a lesson for all of us. Pastors can easily abuse their position and inflict serious emotional, spiritual, and financial damage on other Christians. It is right that we learn from these failures. It is right that we put in place safeguards that limit the ability of these wolves in sheep's clothing from abusing people in this way. However, the high-profile cases can distract from the reality that most pastors are godly men who deeply love their people and want nothing more than for the Lord Jesus to be glorified in the lives of the Christians in their churches.

The pastors that I know are humble, godly men who all have failings and imperfections but love their churches and desire to see the Lord glorified. The majority of them are under significant pressure, much of which comes from the behavior and unrealistic expectations of the Lord's people.

A Pastor Writes:

It's lockdown. I've been pouring myself out for our church for months in hours and ways most will never see. I'm exhausted. Many of our older members express appreciation and ask about my welfare, but sadly, younger families seem to consider the pastor to be just a service provider. If the pastor can't provide, perhaps there's another at a church down the road who can. As we limped into "return to church," with its complexity and planning for the remaining weeks of the year (as well as managing some meltdowns), I explained via a survey that there wouldn't be an evening children's program for the seven weeks leading to Christmas—we simply didn't have enough volunteer leaders willing to serve. I get that they are tired; I am truly empathetic. But we were still able to provide a thriving children's ministry in the mornings. What happened next was a series of phone calls behind the scenes until the grumbling was vocalized at a parish council meeting. I couldn't believe we were having this conversation. Despite the hardship of the year, providing relational support, care, and cohesion; online services that some didn't even bother to try or just skipped through; the constant communication and updates that went unopened;

the lack of a day off for months; the run of funerals; the marriage that required intervention for six tearful weeks that no one else knew about; the continual exhortation to care and wait for one another as a church through anxious vaccination discussions, suddenly I was now being beaten up over consumer-driven disappointment—folks who didn't get all they had hoped for. I was so flat I went to bed with self-pity and the fantasy of quietly emailing my resignation and disappearing to a river somewhere to read the Psalms and leaving them to it. I woke at two and didn't get back to sleep until sometime after three, having had the classic anxiety dreams. I drifted back to sleep until the five thirty alarm woke me. It was time to meet my early Bible study and encourage them.

What I have tried to do in this book is help us as Christian people, as congregation members, to understand some of the pressures our pastors are under, and to encourage us to be more intentional and loving in how we relate to them. We need to realize that we can make a significant difference to our pastor's ability to do ministry, and so to the health of our church, by actively supporting him—in our prayers, encouragement, listening, giving, forgiving, submitting, and handling of accusations. We need to be careful, thoughtful, and biblical as we relate to our pastor in each of these areas. We often think of how our pastor relates to us: Does he preach good sermons that I find helpful? Does he support me in my Christian life? Does he do enough to justify my giving? There may be a place for those questions, but the Christian life is about loving other people—including our pastor. And so we should ask: Do I pray for him, encourage him, listen to him, give generously, forgive, submit, and make sure that accusations are dealt with biblically?

In the end, this book sounds a call to abandon a passive, consumerist model of church. It calls us to abandon the notion that the pastor performs the ministry, which we evaluate according to how it benefits us. It is a call to reject the error that he is our once-a-week religious entertainment provider. It is a call to abandon the idea that he is our spiritual guru, who will drop everything any time we need him. It is a call for us all to be devoted to the work of the Lord. It is a call for us to love and support our pastor. It is a call to fight for him!

Appendix 1

What If I Differ with My Pastor on Politics?

POLITICS IS DIVISIVE. That has always been the case, but probably now more than ever. A common cause of tension between pastors and congregation members is a perception that a pastor does not strongly enough endorse a particular political position or takes the wrong political stance. The COVID pandemic has made this tension particularly acute in the last couple of years—political discussion has come into the church in the shape of disagreements on church closures, mask mandates, and vaccines. But it was present before and will be present after the pandemic. The 2016 and 2020 US elections were also points of tension, with Christians divided on who they should vote for.

What should you do if you differ with your pastor politically? What should you do if you differ with him strongly? I have read more than one Christian commentator argue that Christians should leave their church if a pastor takes or fails to take a particular stance.

This book is published by a US publisher, and I currently live in Australia. I am not qualified to comment on US politics and how the church should operate there. But I grew up somewhere with arguably a more divided political scene than the United States—Northern Ireland. The intersection between the church and the political scene when I was growing up in the 1980s was acute. To be a Protestant Christian was to have a particular view of the relationship between Northern Ireland and the rest of the United Kingdom and the Republic of Ireland. Most Protestant Christians wanted (and still want) to remain part of the United Kingdom. Most Roman Catholics wanted to reunite with the Republic of Ireland. As such, Protestants saw the Christian political stance as wanting to remain part of the United Kingdom. For a church to deny or even downplay this desire was seen as tantamount to lining up with Roman Catholicism. Pressure was put on ministers to speak on this issue from the pulpit, to allow special services celebrating Northern Ireland's British heritage, and to even display British flags in church.

Most pastors resisted saying things from the pulpit. However, what do you do about displaying flags in church and holding special services? To do so would make it very hard for any Roman Catholic ever to come into your church. Therefore, many pastors would not allow these things to occur in their churches—for the sake of the gospel.

My hope is that, if you have political differences with your pastor, that you will be understanding and see the complexity in the issues at hand. It is rare that there is absolute certainty on either side. Even if you have come to a firm conviction, you need to understand that your pastor may have other people in his ear telling him that he should take the other position. Sometimes it is a case of the pastor being a coward and failing to take a stand; other times he simply wants to care for people in the midst of a genuinely confusing world.

If you decide that for everyone's sake it is better to leave the church—and you may—you should be godly in the way that you do it (see appendix 2). But there is a case for letting some things go. Not *every* political issue is a primary issue. Suppose your pastor refuses to publicly call people to support a particular presidential candidate. Is that really a primary issue? Is that a reason to leave a church?

You may disagree with your pastor's approach on a particular issue. He could be wrong. You could be wrong. It *may* be important enough to leave. It *may* not. In any case, the way to proceed is with grace, patience, and forgiveness.

The "A Pastor Writes" sidebar below illustrates some of the complexity. You may read this and be frustrated with my pastor friend for compromising one way or another. But I hope reading it at least helps you see the complexity around these issues as pastors work out how to care for people in their churches with very different opinions.

A Pastor Writes:

I've had people say I'm offensive and hurtful because I'm OK with vaccines, and they have threatened to withdraw membership from our church. Others have said that we are capitulating, like churches did in Nazi Germany. On the other side of this, I have vaccinated people who want more Christians in our church to get vaccinated so we can enjoy more freedom. Both sides want me to say something from the pulpit, but my conviction is that I preach Christ from the pulpit. If I lose this conviction, I fear I'll lose myself.

Appendix 2

When and How Should
I Leave a Church?

WHAT CIRCUMSTANCES WOULD COMPEL a person to leave a church? How should the departure be undertaken?

There are two reasons to leave a church. First, the church is actively teaching people to believe or live in ways contrary to the gospel. This is, in some ways, the more straightforward reason. You cannot continue to sit under a ministry that is teaching against God's word or promoting an ungodly lifestyle. Of course, in practice, it is not always so easy. No two Christians would agree on every matter of doctrine.

Paul can speak of certain gospel truths as "of first importance" (1 Cor. 15:3). To deny these truths (e.g., the death of Christ for sins or his physical, bodily resurrection) would be to deny the gospel. Similarly, Paul states that anyone who preaches a "different gospel" (Gal. 1:6) than the apostolic gospel he preached is "accursed" (Gal. 1:8–9). There are truths that a person cannot deny without denying the gospel, and the New Testament is clear in its condemnation. However, there are other truths that Paul as an apostle of Christ articulates with Christ's authority and that he thinks "mature" Christians should accept, but he nevertheless can say to the Philippians that "if in anything you think otherwise, God will reveal that also to you" (Phil. 3:15). He is not saying that he could be wrong, but he recognizes that not every Christian is as mature as he is. Here, then, is a difference of opinion that does not lead to condemnation or splitting. Similarly, some actions require exclusion from Christian fellowship (1 Cor. 5:1–5), whereas others generate acceptable disagreement, such as whether Christians should eat meat (Rom. 14:1–13). As long as Christians do not despise or judge their brothers and sisters, both approaches have a place. So we need to consider if a matter is so central that we *have* to leave.

Second, however, I also think that a case can be made that while you might be free to stay at a particular church, it might be best for you and for the pastor if you leave, particularly if your ongoing presence at the church would be detrimental to your own or others' godliness. It is more important for you to regularly meet with God's people and be encouraged than for you to remain at a church that causes bitterness of heart. Of course, you could abuse this freedom to justify jumping around like those Paul speaks of who "having itching ears . . . will accumulate for themselves teachers to suit their own passions" (2 Tim. 4:3). But my assumption is that, if you have read this far, you are a godly Christian who would make this decision prayerfully and carefully.

How should you leave? Avoid the extremes of slinking off without saying anything or storming off while throwing your complaints at anyone who will listen. Like anything you do in the Christian life, leaving a church should be done with prayerfulness and love. Hopefully, by this stage you will have had a number of conversations with your pastor, and your leaving will not be a surprise to him. It will not necessarily be easy, but you are not turning away from Christ: you are transferring from one fellowship to another. While it should not be done lightly, there is not actually a scriptural command to prevent you from doing that.

Acknowledgments

A NUMBER OF PEOPLE generously gave time to help me write this book. I am grateful to Andrew Agnew, Andrew Bruce, Adam Ch'ng, Leo Davison, Jonny Gibson, Ben Gray, Russ Grinter, Reuben Hunter, Lee Murray, Emma Orr, Andrew Price, Paul Ritchie, Rory Shiner, Geoff Thompson, Jason Veitch, and Duncan Woods. Philip Kern gave detailed feedback, for which I am especially grateful. Thank you to Andrew Moody and the Gospel Coalition Australia for their encouragement to publish the article that led to this book.

Thank you to the team at Crossway and especially Greg Bailey for help with editing.

To the pastors this book is dedicated to (as to many others): I thank God for your faithful service, which has been a blessing to me and so many. Keep going!

General Index

Scripture Index